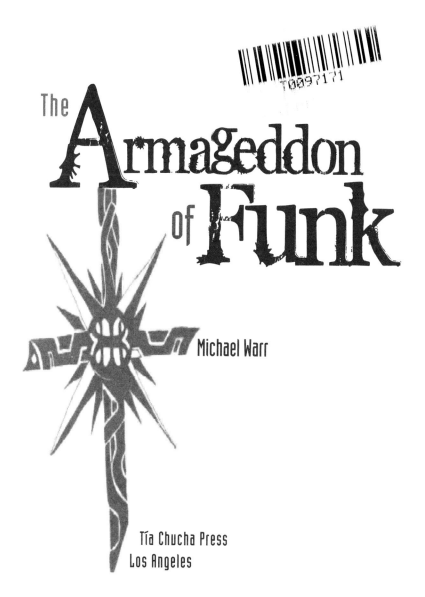

The Armageddon of Funk

Michael Warr

Tía Chucha Press
Los Angeles

Printed in the United States.

ISBN 978-1-882688-42-5

Book design: Jane Brunette
Cover art by Tony Fitzpatrick entitled "The Oil Beast."

Published by:

Tia Chucha Press
A Project of Tia Chucha's Centro Cultural, Inc.
PO Box 328
San Fernando, CA 91341
www.tiachucha.com

Distributed by:

Northwestern University Press
Chicago Distribution Center
11030 South Langley Avenue
Chicago, IL 606028

Tia Chucha Press is the publishing wing of Tia Chucha's Centro Cultural, Inc., a 501 (c) 3 nonprofit corporation. Tia Chucha's Centro Cultural has received funding for this book from the National Endowment for the Arts. Other funding for Tia Chucha's Centro Cultural's programming and operations has come from the California Arts Council, Los Angeles County Arts Commission, Los Angeles City Department of Cultural Affairs, The California Community Foundation, the Annenberg Foundation, the Weingart Foundation, National Association of Latino Arts and Culture, Ford Foundation, MetLife, Southwest Airlines, the Andy Warhol Foundation for the Visual Arts, the Thrill Hill Foundation, the Middleton Foundation, Center for Cultural Innovation, Not Just Us Foundation, John Irvine Foundation, and The Guacamole Fund, among others. Donations have also come from Bruce Springsteen, John Densmore of the Doors, Jackson Browne, Lou Adler, Richard Foos, Adrienne Rich, Tom Hayden, Dave Marsh, Mel Gilman, Jack Kornfield, Jesus Trevino, David Sandoval, Gary Stewart, Denise Chavez and John Randall of the Border Book Festival, and Luis & Trini Rodriguez, as well as others.

TABLE OF CONTENTS

Gwendolyn, Velvet Lounge, Mensch

Ouija Boards, Chocolat, Magnolias

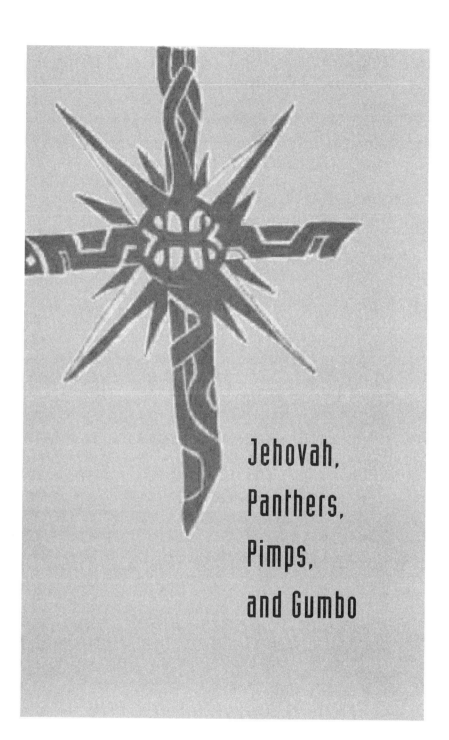

Jehovah,
Panthers,
Pimps,
and Gumbo

My Father's Favorite Pastime

To Tony Fitzpatrick

On edge of the darkest ghetto
stood Candlestick Park
lit bright as an A-bomb's flash.

With tiny hands I turned
a Bazooka-scented baseball card
of Willie Mays. Rows of shattering
batting stats dispersed into smoke,
while Willie stuck like skin,
unforgettably black like my Mother,
whose schoolmates called "Shinola."

Black like her son,
who Abyssinians would one day
adopt as "red black."

In the shadow of America's
spectacle still nothing mattered
but Blackness. Against the night's
cruel chill we huddled against the
Hawk, sipping Ghirardelli chocolate,
in search of baseball's hearth.

Fat with peanuts and Crackerjacks,
a white man sold us something
silver, shiny, wallet-shaped.

Wrapping it in a velvet pouch,
deep blue and fit for royalty,
my Father handed me the mystery,

warmer than a Sunday oven,
bringing mad joy to my hands.
I kept that warmer for centuries,
in an unlocked chaotic drawer.

Packed with memories, junk,
imagination, the blaze in its metal guts
stealing even Willie's thunder.

Then He Became One

A bulky blur, he stormed through our bedroom,
in the living room, resurrecting us from the dead.

Tracing wet footsteps to the bathtub we found our
mother's *Watchtowers* and *Awakes* floating.
Pages of holy literature, our father baptized before
leaving for work, bled ink from their watery grave.

We were hidden away that day. Sequestered in the
Bayview as religious refugees. Living out of bulging
luggage in clandestine cells of believers.

He was never far away. We rode slowly by his
chrome-laden hog parked outside the Chinese grocery.
We watched as he bought non-family food. He could
not see us scratching at car windows to be with him.

We recited scriptures he did not know. Repenting
out of shame, duty and devotion, he became a Bible
toting zealot. We returned from our exodus, attending
Kingdom Hall together, the model monotheistic unit.

Often I prayed that he had remained a heathen.

The Armageddon of Funk (1965/2006)

IN MEMORY OF JAMES BROWN

"The one thing that can solve most of our problems is dancing."
                    —THE GODFATHER OF SOUL

Watts rebels. A tethered cosmonaut "walks" in space.
T.S. Elliot, Nat King Cole, and Sir Winston Churchill die.
Malcolm is murdered. The "Grateful Dead" is born.
Sekou Sese Mobuto steals and sells the Congo.
Che crosses Lake Tanganyika as "Tatu" to take it back.
Ginsberg Howls, speaking "flower power" in the city
where I first imagine. The entire Northeastern United States
blacks out. The Voting Rights Act is passed. U.S. troops
deploy to Da Nang, Vietnam. Gang of Four ascends.

My only worry, at ten years old, is what will happen to
the world *if* James Brown dies?

Monks rebel. Pluto is no longer a planet. The sun eclipses.
Robert Creeley, Coretta Scott King, and the King of Tonga
die. Monks are murdered in Myanmar. The Dead still
play live. Congo holds its first "true" elections since Patrice
Lumumba's assassination. Howl turns fifty. Jack Hirschman,
communist, is Poet Laureate of the city where I first imagined.
Deadliest heat wave since the Dust Bowl plagues Midwest.
Voting Rights are extended another inadequate quarter.
Saddam Hussein hanged. Forbidden City evicts Starbucks.

Man Within the Boy

...for there is no man that does not sin....
— KINGS 8:46

I stumbled on unsuspected flesh,
a woman wrapped in black fishnet,
looking up from pages of a private
detective magazine buried deep in
in his station wagon's sunken trunk,
under cans of oil and tarnished tools.
My flash of fascination lost in loyalty
to the secret him, aware at that age of
Father worship, that if he could sin, then
all men sinned. Our tacit treaty stored
away with soldering irons and caulking
guns, trowels and levers, obscuring
the nuts and bolts of us.

During The Station Wagon Incident
my hair exploded in noisy disruption
of familial bliss in the battle zone of the
family Ford, me worried about my "do,"
a sculpture I'd chiseled myself, each
stony strand in palatial grounds precision.
Not mere hair, but an afro-lutionary
manifesto to raised fists sheathed in black
leather gloves in Mexico City, occupying
an altitude high enough for a world of white
to see it could not divert black cyclones
from hurling attitude against oppression.
Punching America in its two faces.
My 'fro a bomb of symbolism my father
wanted to defuse, countering Black Power

with rows of negro-tillery against style he
could not contain or understand. His throat
spraying a disgusted volley of "sissy." The
backseat igniting with the slur, scorching
my insurrectionary hair, dissipating in the
nuclear atmosphere never to be heard again.

In the muted aftermath I would never
know if "The Man Who Knew Everything,"
from Corinthians to pouring concrete,
followed as Gloria led me far from Jehovah's
flock to a spot secluded from believers and
sheltered by the fairground's abandoned stage.
She pinned me flat – a blacklight poster against
the wall. Then he pedaled by. I caught him
in the edge of my eye, pretending we sinners
were not there, so thrilled to see his "sissy"
sinning, that Gloria became an angel
with lips for wings.

He would forgive the treason of a kiss,
but never the blasphemy of blackness.
At our once tranquil dinner table he became
Negro and I was Black. Protest grew
from the roots in my scalp, to the tip of my
tongue, from our dining room to a coliseum,
where 16,000 Christian followers voted as
one on some rhetorically righteous question,
all speaking the preordained answer –
a unified, sheepish, "yes."
Yet from a nearly front-row mountaintop,
with revolutionary hair glistening,
I shouted "no." The vote 15,999 to one.
My tongue recruited to the vanguard.
My "cousin" choking on a swallowed laugh.
My "counter-revolutionary" father

sitting too far away to launch
a pre-emptive slap in fear of what I might
do next. His stare a skin-disintegrating
beam of light from the Ark of the Covenant.
My brain on fire. Expecting execution.
My model family, awaiting its place
in Paradise, sitting in stunned silence.
A notch against us in heaven.
A notch against me on earth.
No "Wild Wild West," no "Monkees,"
or "Star Trek" for three months.

No Uhura?

Now my father was Mussolini...

Crossing the Bay Bridge and Other Expanses

Slow dancers must be eighteen inches apart.
— EDICT FROM THE WATCHTOWER BIBLE AND TRACT SOCIETY

On the Oakland side of the Bay witnesses stealthily rebelled,
never measuring the space between their sacrilegious mounds.
Outside their Kingdom Halls, non-believers tossed Molotovs,
strapped semi-automatic weapons across their stylishly leathered
chests, while nipping proudly at the "pinkish," rotund, trigger
happy, pillars of the State.

Grinding was emancipation on the freshly coated concrete floor
of a black-lighted garage, leaving me stung and "stupid-minded."
Wondering how Sheila could make the groove in her body so hard,
so soft, so hard, so good. Goodness my father warned me of one
nearly idyll San Francisco afternoon, before this kind of magic
blossomed, as we quietly brushed our house canary yellow.

His abrupt caution to "keep your hands above the covers" ended
our synchronous strokes of unspoken "manly" glee forever.
I nodded in confused, hollow, agreement. Hands? Who needs hands
for happiness? We never painted as one or spoke of simple things
bound intricately to "sin" again. After Sheila "goodness" mattered.
The pheromones of illicit garage grinding permanently steeped.

Safe in the tranquility of my mother's kitchen I asked her
"How a girl could move that way."

Deuteronomy Says Die

FOR JEAN BESHEARS HUMPHREY,
1952-2006

Within the celestial walls of Intensive Care,
in our divinity's eternal glare, my sister, dilated
and dying, suffered from a literal interpretation:

Any soul who eats any blood, that soul
must be cut off from his people.

Refusal became a kamikaze act dispatched
swiftly through defiance of scientific dogma
or slowly through *Yahweh's* wrath.

Lost in prayer, caught in corporeal hell,
certain to join their daughter in "heaven-on-earth"
our parents would not sign the blooding papers.

Jean obeyed both of her omnipotent Fathers.
Her "too soon child" would live even if she died.
Jehovah became "their" God that night.

Manchild

In the beginning I read *Manchild in the Promised Land*
for the sex. For the fascination with whores.

I had a long-distance rapport with whores
from the rolled-down window of my brother's first car.
A black Buick cruising through the Fillmore where he
educated me in the fine art of distinguishing between
the two T's – trim and transvestite.

Lessons learned in the underworld of the Tenderloin
where souls where saved by heroines officially decked
in rabbit-fur capes, but always in fishnet-stockings,
platforms and psychedelic mini-skirts, spreading their
gospel within earshot of the men who owned, sweet-talked,
beat them. To us they were ex-slaves that had "gotten over."

When not pretending to be "The Temptations," singing
in the echo chamber known as the boys bathroom,
we all wanted to be pimps. Pimps and gangsters.
We worshipped Al Capone. I drew his portrait and sold it
at lunch to pay for butter cookies. The sugar did not make
me soft. I still wanted to be a gangster. A something "Slim."
A "Red" something. A "Detroit" something. A "Chicago"
something. As long as it was "Slim."

We dreamed of gangster leaning like Super Fly in suede
Eldorados. Like that chocolate-brown Cadillac, sometimes
parked on Divisadero, somehow covered in a coat of suede
we dared not touch for fear of being shot by the owner.

Until we had a "Caddy" of our own we wore pimp shades,
pimp stripes, pimps socks, copped a pimp 'tude, walked the
pimp walk in pink walking suits, stepped with a pimp beat,
carrying a walking stick with Isaac Hayes and Curtis Mayfield
playing in the background. Sliding and dragging our bad foot
like a cool Quasimodo leaning towards Mecca. Wearing fake
alligator shoes, stolen Timex watches, and party jewelry.
Our brims slanted to the side. Our minds slanted towards
the pits of pimpdom.

Then Malcolm Little, Detroit Red, escaped pimpdom,
carrying a dictionary instead of a walking stick, escaped
the social prison that offered only broken careers and broken
heroes: gangster or pimp, prisoner or cadaver. Outside the
schoolyard Black Panthers hawked papers crying "pig, pig, pig,
kill the pigs, pigs, pigs."

Now I drew portraits of Huey in that Wicker Throne
and "Manchild" took on another meaning.

The First Time Ever...

In my '68 Volvo, on a sloping street outside the house
where I taught myself Bach preludes, danced the James Brown
and Calypso while my mother tried to waltz me, where she
allowed my zoo of beetles, frogs and ladybugs bottled in her
living room, outside that museum of my youth, a Colombian
revolutionary escaped from the bucket seat, leaned across the
stick shift, and strapped me into first love with a kiss.

Our eyes flared across enlightened rooms, crowded with cadre,
in picturesque Victorian Flats in San Francisco's Mission,
where the Symbionese Liberation Army and "Squeaky" Fromm
fabricated faulty solutions. At her antique dining table we shared
utopian Super Burritos from *Las Palmas,* near the *Panaderia*
and Maoist bookstore, blared music to deny the FBI our whispered
strategy and tactics, studied Vladimir's *What Is To Be Done?*
as the Isley Brothers' *Who's That Lady?* spun conspiratorially.

On a couch in my boyhood bedroom in front of a window
she would not notice until we too were wide open, all the
dialectical discussions were lost in the tearing off of clothes,
as I told her "I wanted first to read a book on how to do it,
so that I would do it right." She kept tearing off her clothes,
not letting her husband, *dos niños,* or my 19-year-old naivety
distract her 29-year-old wisdom.

I quit the Bank of America's promise of a perfect bourgeois
future to be a full-time functionary, taut from pseudo
unemployment, stomach flat as a stack of Leninist leaflets.
On the way to meetings she slipped her hand into my
baggy pants and pulled slightly as I shifted gears.

Back to Baton Rouge

Last time I crushed
this blackened soil,
Roy Rogers was my hero.
I squatted and painted
rocks red with nail polish,
the green ice from a Dixie Cup
dripping down my chin.
My Grandfather
black as an eclipse,
his Choctaw hair shining,
his rusty carpenter hands
twisting chicken necks at breakfast.
My Great Aunt's farm smothered
in shade and Magnolias.
My Father's sky-blue Continental,
its imperialistic grinning grill
splattered with the state of Texas.
My baby sister peeing
beside the car.

That was Louisiana.

A jar of pickled pig lips
reminds me where I come from.
Where gumbo ain't nouveau cuisine.
And folks in every parish
affectionately call me cuz,
bridging the Baptist/'hovah schism
that blocked our childhood dance.
I am prodigal returning to root,
PowerBook in tow.

Out of place. Embraced.
My Frisco/Chi-Town/Addis
twang mixing with their twang.
They curl "yes ma'am,"
to my West-Coasted mother.
Our lips won't form the sound,
the Louisiana in us too far gone.

Uncle Alton, not seen since seven,
asks "is poetry making money?"
They say this is a Creole thing.
It doesn't matter.
I envy my uncle's name.
I covet all their names.
Names worthy of phat novels.
My Father Alcide.
My Mother Gaynell.
My Willie Mae and Bessie aunts.
Our roots so thick and gritsy.
Our names circumcised,
our assimilation so invisible,
only the "Lee's" and "Elwood's"
thrust between them cling
to the southern soil.

I am of this land yet lost.
An immigrant in old country.
Only the gumbo feels like home.

Scars

I.

David cheats the would-be assassin aiming at his heart.
Inevitably he parades the spoils of his triumphant crusades.
Flags sway unfurled atop his captured chest –
the fleshy, heroic, cartography of uncharted excavation.

I see a twisted type of medal carved across the naked
terrain of this people's poet laureate. I feel the lifeline ripped
from his calf and spliced *en su enorme corazon* as if
"Liquid Thoughts" coursed through my pulsing rivers.

I caress the scars of my mentor.

II.

Colonel Girma arrived armed with everything
but immortality.

I never asked "how, or when, or from where" he was marred.

The map sculpted on his gladiator jaw
led to the unexpected –taxis shared with goats; a stark
interrogation cell; dim, covert, rooms of the revolution's
most wanted; the blackest of black-rose petal goddesses
waiting for him at home; and seaside warfronts
matted in the horrid wake.

III.

Cristina bore the rapist's crude signature across
the rim of her lip, slit first to terrorize, then paralyze,

and finally to forever remind. Even freedom fighters
feel torment slashing beneath their stoic surface.

She was the same and not the same. She still spoke
through fuchsia petals in my boyish eyes. She could not be
silenced by any knife.

Not knowing how or where to look, or what to do or say,
possessing no incantations other than fledging poetry

I wrote "…your scar makes you who you are."

IV.

Karen carries a diagram of our childhood
scraped onto her adolescent ankle. The spokes
of our brother's bicycle left her branded. For what?
The thrill of a "look no hands moment?"

I've stored the shrieking and the trauma. I see her hanging
to Jerome's waist. I've forgotten the "how." Precisely why
the letting go happened.

How does a foot even enter a spinning wheel? I could ask her,
except we barely talk. We who innocently babbled our own
secret sibling Pig Latin.

I crave science to explain such an unlikely feat – like Lake Kiva
settled in Africa's Great Rift Valley exploding inexplicably.
How did it happen? The foot affair? What was the foot
to gear ratio? The objective conditions? The Hegelian "nodal line"?
A foot miniscule enough to fit? A wheel massive enough
to mangle? A modicum of distraction from the sibling sideline?

I shiver at the memory and search for the right moment to ask.

Not Even the San Joaquin...

To Patricia Zamora

At nature's intervals of light and darkness you are missing.

I may seem unaware as other voices, words, obsessions and
untamed terms for the next completion clutter what I breathe.
These are simply everyday cessations. You are ever flowing.
Where you normally fly, circle, land, and create inside me
seems empty until at least I hear your song.

"Missed" is too mundane a word. In truth you are never gone.

You are spun into what I am made of and so you are with me.
Missed but not missing. Your absence measured in change.
A part of Chicago stolen. My motion reduced to one room.
My wanderings alone. My days adrift. My balance spent.
You bring the invincible joy that escapes me.

Love" is too mundane a word. Still I speak it. To you.

Within this stuttering, unromantic, uttering is my devotion.
The reach of your radiance is endless. It spans continents.
So we are near in this dictatorship of distance. Still I want
to be not merely near you but with you.

With no valleys between our warmth.

Street Signs, Convolutions, and other California Coincidences

I.

Somehow the bus driver drove his mammoth
rush-hour machinery into my father's head,
dropping him to the Market Street asphalt
dazed, but not yet dead. His "high-yella" body
sprawled momentarily. His mind stuck at work
keying sales into the old-school register on
Levin's Auto Supply's thick-glass counter.

II.

On a Chicago boulevard lined in conspiring
trees, the street signs that surround us sing
"California," "Sacramento," "Richmond," and
"Francisco." A sturdy, sunburnt, graying man
cutting the rowdy grass outside the corner church,
says he too is called "Francisco." I say it is also
the name of my wife's late brother.

III.

In the Volvo, on the way to Zion, Illinois,
we wear out Jose Feliciano's song.
He is not the only Californian dreaming.

IV.

In Patricia's mind Livingston is Shangri-La,
twenty minutes outside Modesto, California.
She picks grapes sweet with sunshine from

a meandering bunch enveloping a neighbor's
mailbox. Another neighbor, from India, brings
a basket of blue chicken eggs and remembers
the bucket of tangerines her father Rufino
handed him over a fence he'd built himself.

V.

Twenty years after the crippled smile froze
to the left side of my father's stroke-shaped face,
I unknowingly arrive where Levin's once stood,
a lustrous temple of cultural philanthropy,
where spark plugs, tail pipes and distributor caps
once hung from the walls, creativity is prominently
displayed, shuffled, rejected, sustained, and
I sell art where my father sold auto parts.

Congas Over Marin County

Leaking loudly from a golden-dreaded drummer, erratic beats
splutter through the translucent Jacuzzi swirl of Mill Valley.

Stunned briefly in a draping canopy of leaves the notes ricochet
wildly off reddish roof tiles of the Piazza D'Angelo.

A streak of sinewy arms subsumes tones as deep as the wails
of whales and high as the cries of wrens.

Cacophony slows as the Kangol-lidded drummer finds his groove
in genetically coded markers of the musically evolved multitude.

The talking book flares and calms. Harmonics emerge out of the
grating, discordant, and incomprehensible.

Freed from the oppression of homogeneity his opaque fingers
flash against the conga's metal-flaked ruby torso.

A message emanates from the eon-weathered African membrane
expanding in northern rays of enlightenment.

A feather-headed child is danced like an ethereal marionette
inside the safeguarding scaffolding of her father.

Termites,
Stalin Mau-Mau,
Timbuktu

A Naivety Scene

Spinning in careening circles. Tires screeching lines of black
script on gray pavement. Outside the Lion of Judah's Jubilee Palace,
one minute after midnight, the hour militia guards shoot at cars
moving subversively without military plates, Major Girma drives
madly to welcome and assumingly orientate me.

Down the secluded, narrow, muddy roads past "Diplomats Row"
a villa's walls are lined with bottles and bodies of women in aura.
Glass and flesh an array of shapes, shades, and silhouettes. In the
obfuscating lounge lighting everyone seems headless like ancient
severed statues. Stepping into sight the women come to holistic life.
A blue-black, braided, "gift" from Major Girma is "given" for my
unwrapping with the rugged warning it is "rude to refuse."

Aged in scotch and honey wine, my debauchery is a stuttered blur.
The villa has faded into Eucalyptus trees. The blue-black beauty
is no longer headless. She is beside me in the Major's car.
He must be giving her a ride. I am outside my apartment's gate.
He must be letting me off first. She is standing at the gate
beside me. Major Girma is laughing, repeating, "don't be rude,"
before speeding into the missing night. We are naked. Her English
speaks only body parts. She does not like what I like.

A miserable silence consumes us until curfew slithers away.
Morning, a drunken intruder, stumbles across the room as
the beauty of blue-black skin unfolds her hand. She can say
"seventy-five dollars" perfectly. I am temporarily disabled
by disbelief. I demand my money back the next day —

from Girma.

Plotting At The Ras Hotel — Addis Ababa

To Tesfarmariam

In cafe clouds of *Nyala* smoke,
over espresso cups of *bunna watet*
and frosted glasses of *Melotti* beer,
Embassy, Jomo and Stalin Mau-Mau,
Zimbabwean liberation fighters, spar
with Captain Getachew's air force crew,
all cursing Mobuto, reciting Nkrumah,
while dissecting the seizure of power.
Switching between Shona, Ndebele,
and Portuguese, they respectfully
speak the King's English for me.

A survivor of cluster bombs and
green tracer bullets, Embassy advises
"it is harder for a fighter jet to mow
you down if you lie flat on the ground."

Jomo survived — his stomach pierced
by U.S.-South African-Israeli shrapnel,
but he can never eat *foufou* again.
He lost pieces of his small intestines
for Rhodesia to become Zimbabwe.
He wonders if an American would
ever give up the jingoistic joy of
Quarter Pounders With Cheese to
change more than their country's name,
to lose even half a pound of history's
most enormous gut.

Jomo never knew Tadesse,

who could no longer plot at the Ras.
By law his house enchained him.
He cheated these chains at midnight,
risking what was left of his life,
sneaking across the Akaki River to
my Addis apartment to share the
truth inside his forced solitude
so that I ... *Would Explain A Few Things*
to inject visibly into *Open Veins.*

To be like Tadesse I taunted the
wrath of the "New Flower's" curfew,
tempted the steel of bayoneted M-16s
wielded by newly empowered peasants,
respected and feared Tesfamariam,
who taught me to capture answers
with out questions — my friend the spy
seized by other spies, and lost
inside a pitch-black, Asmara cell,
isolated, blinded, still sheds light —

 "After our enemy, your enemy
is our greatest enemy. Overthrow
the ugly one. Your own."

Addis Ababa means "New Flower" in Amharic.

The Vulnerable

A fat bag of fresh bread
for this last Ethiopian dollar.
It is snowing in Addis Ababa,
where it never snows. Snowing
black clouds of white
termites. Their fallen wings
pave the unpaved earth.

They are vulnerable in their insect
dance, assaulted by daggers of rain.
Chickens gorge on their helplessness.
Dragonflies feast on their termite flesh.
Children chase them down, pluck
their wings before they descend,
as they would if left to their nature.

Like nightfall the female's wings
flutter swiftly to a grassy, frenzied,
bed of euphoria. Where she falls she
makes more swarms, in a dance as
confused as the Creation. Until caught in
the Mediterranean of their insect fog,
where calm overcomes chaos.

They survive.

Revolutionary Eyes

Flower of a summer revolution,
a fearless outcry in her eyes, warning
"First you must get by me."

Famine since ninth century,
fed by endless war, flame is
mirrored in her gaze, cataclysmic
change courses through her veins.

She is the restoration of generations
three millennia after rigor mortis.
She is Abyssinia raised from dead.

She is hunger's executioner.

Stealing Souls

After
the American's
distortion, with
a simple flip
of aperture,
her backdrop
signed itself Monet
and faded into poverty.
The French Impressionism
she never knew
taunted behind her back.
She suspected evil
from the *ferenge's* extended eye
and resisted the invasion
into her mind,
territory he thought
seizable when unable
to conquer her country.
She had weaved
trenches of braids
around her crown
and rifled down
his advances.

On the Way to Timbuktu

You cannot fly without radar
when the desert clouds the sky.
                    — MALIAN PILOT

Moments outside of Bamako,
above the sepia-tinted town,
an arid ocean anarchically undulates
below my cloudy oval window
in waves formed by a nascent storm.
Shards of crystallized history, swept
into the sky, beat against the silver jacket
of our pitiful plane, like enraged rain,
humbling us to the African ground.

A rickety radio shack, fruit stand,
and bench, line the leveled landing strip.
The flat, hot, golden universe engulfs us.
Raindrops filled with grains of sand,
swept up by the storm we wait to subside,
smear the "hieroglyphics" in my notes,
dissolving sentences into faded arteries.

Circling above Timbuktu, we confront
the twisted, charred, and aged remains
of a Soviet fighter plane, forced humbly
again to the African ground, signaling a
warning, inadvertently, its once menacing
metal carcass strewn across the runway,
half buried in the encroaching sand
dancing around emasculated weaponry
as if celebrating a victory.

Desert Lost (Leaving Timbuktu)

Choked on petrol spiked with water,
by traders at Timbuktu, our Land Rover dies
in the desert, where Exxon is an illusion.

A barren landscape shape shifts into trees
as hologrammed-Africans wave us into the
inferno on foot.

The Malian driver conjures parts from
detritus of the desert and mystically makes
this heap of metal and *meshugaas* work, until
even his mechanical healing succumbs
to the conquest of sun and sand.

The Englishman in our crew breaks down too,
into a whimpering disaster film cliché, afraid
that "tall white people dehydrate faster"
than small black ones closer to lowly nature.
The "Dark Continent" would not devour him.

A battered lorry, its flatbed crammed with
disbelieving desert people, comes to our rescue
for a take-it-or-die-in-the-boiling-Sahara price.

Waterless, hungry and out of place, we arrive
in Bela. Three brightly tie-dyed village girls,
draped in orange, green and black, watch our
emergence from desolation and trace our steps
around their monochrome town of mud, asking:

"Why do you walk in the terrifying sun
without water, you silly foreign men?"

Pounding in Mali

Obsidian arms
savannah smooth
smash grain
into African atoms
to swallow.

Wooden
accelerators
break matter down
into beats between
polyrhythms.

Visions of
Malian women
elongated
their splendor blazing
and illuminated.

Towers of grace
they encircle the West
that erodes their village
pounding ancient particles
into quarks of song.

To See or Not to See [Zimbabwe Was Once Rhodesia]

I saw Robert Mugabe, President of Zimbabwe, driving a
"Flash" taxi by "Vee Vee's African Restaurant" in Uptown,
Chicago, where a meal at each backyard reunion must include
something barbequed from every kitchen of the world.

In this United Nations of neighborhoods a guerilla turned
head-of-state, once overthrown, just might weave undetected
through imperialism's circular traffic, wooden beads across
his back, a see-through bulletproof borderline dividing his
imposed seat of exile from his passenger.

He might conceal a Saturday Night Special, more dangerous
these days than the Kalashnikov rifles a freedom fighter once
smuggled to Africa from the fabled Soviet Union long before
this cascading catastrophe after Zimbabweans fought, died,
liberated, signed, cried, waited, waited, waited, and took
promised, undelivered, soil, taking their "40 acres and a mule"
from white estates for power, reparations and enough to eat.

Mugabe – the dictator – is nowhere near Chicago. He lives
among offspring of Cecil Rhodes and Ian Smith, never named
dictators, or even thieves, their control camouflaged in flawed
accords and inheritance. Tainted history holds the most fertile
and desired farmland for ransom from the Africans it belonged
to before the massacres of "discovery," when the dazzling glory
of diamonds, chrome, and gold, blinded world morality,
enabling the massacres we never see.

Gwendolyn,
Velvet Lounge,
Mensch

Which Side of Michigan Avenue Are You On?

She has circled the "Magnificent Mile" pavement outside the
Congress Plaza Hotel too long, recycling chants, labored slogans,
and surrogate food stamps.

She survives assaults of American mythology, the strafing runs
of oppressive summers and bitter bombardment of snow and ice.
Ill wind rubs exploitation in under her unsuspicious epidermis
as she spins *ad nauseum* for what others already have.

She aches from re-walking nowhere on this city's most class
contentious avenue, but dreams beyond the suffocating ownership
of this crumbling edifice to a renovated place called "Hope,"
ever since that shiny day a south-side Senator walked briefly
beside her on the thin line between suffering and suffering less.

She has proselytized in change-fractured English that soon he
would settle her nightmare and America's longest active strike,
not realizing that he *is* the Savior, just not hers.

I've Seen Myself In That Alley

I raced pass the ubiquitous dumpster, squatting blowflies
away to the next oozing collection plate of civilized waste.

Yesterday after yesterday I sleepwalked by this common
place fooled by its false emptiness, reducing it to a state of
insignificance, growing more emotionally ignorant, warned
off by the summer stench, the greasy clump of once washed
cloth comforting someone once like you, jittery from
sleeping softly, thinking a cup of coffee luxurious enough
to beg for it's palmed, steaming, blackness, suddenly a path
to visitations of simple fleeting pleasures.

I am just a "once impossible" scenario from sleeping inside
that clump of cloth in this now significant alley.

Where in that cold continuum are you?

Nazar Picks Me Up

When the kiwi-toned Checker pulled up
the gentle-eyed taxi driver, colored muddy
like the pregnant Euphrates, could not resist
saying "you are pure black."

As if in awe of a passing woman
he could never know, the Pakistani carved an
anti-colonial, counter-cultural, instantaneous
memorial to what beauty was taught not to be,
decapitating imperial truisms of purity only
the hue of alabaster — not some "Bitches Brew"
nightmare distorting blonde locks into
an ideological monstrosity and kowtowed
before centuries of defensive hatred.

When he ejected two Brooks-Brothered men
from his ride for their diatribe against Chicago
"niggers," the superiority of more melanin was
not Nazar's point. He thought his wife, the white
professor of Black History, beautiful beyond
Shakespearean, euro-rhetoric, and noted that in
Nordic enclaves of Europe, they, *sans* eyes of blue
and strands of gold, would not be pure enough.

As the Brooks Brothers assured him he was not
a "nigger" and he passionately insisted he was,
this only squared the root of their confusion when
he deserted them in unnamed territory so far away
from their' sub-level of consciousness that they
fell epochs away from speech.

Bus #3 King Drive

"Who are the parents of this garbage?"
She trained her venom toward the hoards
fleeing "The Taste of Chicago."

"How old is this piece of garbage?"
Her pitch reminiscent of the "Exorcist."
She evil-eyed the pretty little black girl
entranced from across the aisle.

Then staccato-like spit out "p i c k a n i n n y."
"Pussy is pussy." Speaking into an invisible
hand-held contraption to her imaginary friend.

Entertained or horrified, the girl's pupils
widened in recognition of something familiar.
Her mother peered blindly straight ahead.

Skeptically, silently, she wagered that this
was just another disturbed public transportation
monarch coming apart in their plastic throne.

Alighting from her seat of power, she gave the
Art Institute the finger, as if to say true insanity
resided in the privileged pinnacles around her.

Hallucinating at the Velvet Lounge

To Malachi Thompson
(Chicago, April 25, 2004)

When Malachi blew his horn
I dreamed of cornbread, yellow
mounds with burnt edges
on the Velvet's culinary altar.
His sharp cut riffs morphed
into squares of cornbread islands,
floating in streams of warm butter,
clinging to the ribs of my memory.
Speaking in trumpet tongues
of passages and uprisings,
ancient pain and "Good Times" jiving,
sacred beats and blues timing,
drive-by crying and signifying,
an opiate inside of oppression:
a cratered chunk of bacon-infused,
sweet potato, chicken-smothered,
maple-pecan, custard-filled,
smackin' cracklin', jalapeno
enflamed, cornbread — the crepe
of the slaves, now sold
at Whole Foods, in this
jazz-drenched town, built
of golden bricks, and smoke
stacks billowing fumes of corn
on the cob and catfish.
My mind lost in music
and metaphysics, reminiscing
the Sunday manna served
beside my mother's succotash.

Her Words

To Gwendolyn Brooks

An archaeologist,
not a lexicologist, figured it
out. The word was a woman.
Mingling among
the Oromos of Ethiopia,
brandishing a painter's
brush in a dig territorially
defined by string,
the archaeologist swept away
ancient crust and sediment
finding language, alive
and agitated, instead
of the fossilized femur
of a long-dead ramapithecus.
Words wrapped in rhythm,
pleasure, knowledge and pain.
Words as sharply defined
as an Ashanti sculpture. Words
of an African dynasty
made of peoples
not restricted to kings.
Words that survived
the Atlantic. Words
that survived Atlanta. Words
that survived migration,
segregation, integration,
and false resolution.
Words worn as bracelets,
amulets and weapons.
Words that were up

long before they were down.
Word Up.
Words that give more
than she has taken.
Children's lives reweaved
first through her poems
and then through their own.
Words that could weave a world.

Gravitas — In Three Movements

For Fred Fine

I.

In the immortal mind
of this World Changer
bottom line was humanity,
      heart.
Breadlines for subsistence
not enough without beauty
riveted into the beams
      of our being
offered to all in reach of his
brilliant, encompassing, sunlight
where would-be World Changers
were taught to slay
the golem of cyclical crisis.

II.

Firebird soaring underground.
Entrenched scholar on frontlines.
Bronze-Star soldier, profound.
Mobilizer of each one of us.
Gardener of consciousness.
Scientific shaman. Maven.
Mentor to masses. Agitator.
Code Breaker. Mensch.
Papillon.
      Frail enough to fly.

III.

Freedom Fighter. Father.
Idea Monger. Immense
enough to leave an imprint
on our communal stone.
Today "Chaos Theory" is true.
The flapping of a butterfly's
wing could create the force
of a hurricane.

Performed in 2005 at the Memorial of Fred Fine to
music composed and performed by Mitar Mitch Covic.

Truth Incinerated

I only get one death. I want it to be a good one.

A man is on fire alongside Chicago's "Flame of the Millennium."
In his orchestrated agony he still is as invisible as the innocents that
litter the battlefield of unbridled democracy.

In ignorant reactions following the implosion of his every nerve
ending in protest of "mass murder," he is dismissed as delusional for
suicide burning in search of a meaningful defense against the crusades
of a dangerously deluded leader.

A human sacrifice would not deter the Decider from his bloody
business plan for record profits at Exxon Mobil. There is machinery
of slaughter and salvation to mass-produce, destroy, and replace.
Barrels of our addictive elixir to conquer. Terrorists and non-terrorists
to not torture. There are the goals of victory to rename, reframe, and
redefine. Flag-draped coffins, "black sites," and leaks to hide.

When self-immolated men are invisible immorality reigns. We are
either with insanity or against it.

Malachi Ritscher is still on fire…

An Open Poem To Clarence Thomas

"…it's high-tech lynching for uppity blacks
who in any way deign to think for themselves."
— CLARENCE THOMAS

To be lynched is not to be castigated by peers, but castrated
by mobs for raping white women that you've never seen.

There are trees in Mississippi watered by the midnight murder
of black men. Trees with barbarism carved into them. Witnesses
of animalistic, primal lynching. Lynching for which there were
no hearings. Lynching that committed instead of hiding crimes.

Lynching is not a cloak to wrap oneself in for the magical return
of blackness after wiping its significance away. To be lynched
is more than a memory.

You know the pigment-controlled psyche. America's sword
of blackness and sexuality. You sit in the seat of a Justice
empowered, unchallenged, enriched, until the break of senility.
If this is being lynched then lynch me. Lynch all of us.

Written in response to the Anita Hill/Clarence Thomas Hearings and for the
theatre performance "What's This In My Coke?"

Poem Inspired By A Crazed Negro Nazi Reciting Hitler's *Mein Kampf* At Spices Jazz Bar

Ignorancia non est argumentum.
Ignorance is no argument.
What does Spinoza know?
Spinoza knows nothing.
Nipples. Nucleic acid. Nada.
Hyenas are hermaphrodites.
I always wanted to say that in a poem.
I always walked in the footsteps of
the Homo habilis on the dark shore
of Lake Turkana. Kenya on the other side
of the Ogaden. The Muslims chewing *chat*,
teeth green with religious ecstasy,
on a train I am not supposed to be on.
It is 70 A.D., the soldiers of General Titus
could not drown the Jewish slaves
in the Dead Sea, even with
boulders tied around their necks.
They were saved by salt. Not Yahweh.
I always wanted to say that.
The Rosicrucians are part of an
Anglo-Axis Masonic plot. Children of the
Cecidomyian Gall Midge devour their mother
from within, leaving a chitinous shell,
like the proletariat eating out capital.
It is better to heal through superstition,
than to be killed in the scientific way —
a rap by Chinese Abbe Huc in another century.
We are deoxyribonucleic acid: adenine, thymine,
guanine, cytosine, and mostly water.
Morpheus and Thanatos were brothers.

DuBois was a bro'tha.
Nature does not make leaps. This is not true.
Natura no facit saltum.
Punctuated equilibria.
Someone had to said it.

To know that we know
what we know, and that we do not know
what we do not know, that is true knowledge.
Confucius knew this.
To the Negro who mimics Nazis,
extermination is never the answer.

Malcolm Is 'bout More Than Wearing a Cap

The problem is not the letter X
or the myriad of emblazoned caps
even worn backward by white boys.
When Arsenio sports a rhinestone-
studded X to match his Armani suit,
I see Malcolm emasculated by fashion.
As if X symbolized a new NBA team
challenging the Pistons, Cavs, and Bulls,
their jerseys blinking "Buy American"
with every slam dunk sponsorship.
Then a sandwich is named Sandwich X,
and a four-wheeler is named Bronco X,
until the substance of X is x'ed out.
A dollar for every X on a cap
can either make a multi-millionaire,
or hopefully help pay for a revolution,
a cry we hear these days almost
as much as we see X's — in America
where all is commodified.

Will X stand for change or
changing what America wears?
As ruling designers alienate
the Malcolm from the X. Separate
the meaning of Malcolm from the
punctuated power of X.
To Malcolm is to do. Your cap
is clean, but Malcolm is 'bout more
than wearing a cap. Your horn rims
impress, but Malcolm is 'bout vision.
Your T-shirt is down, but Malcolm

is 'bout taking over.
Your enemies will also wear the X,
sell the X, sex the X, film the X,
praise the X, record the X, raise the X,
fraternize and buy the X.
Your enemies will never Malcolm the X.
Only we can Malcolm the X.

Warriors

Warriors fall dead around us.
Murdered on corners buying burgers.
Outside White Castle they scramble
for cover. Five-0 squats, poised for attack,
but can't find the source of the gats
and crack. Warriors fall. Their wounds
stain the stairs of their families' homes.

Cracks in the sidewalk channel their blood
to the next killing. The killings. The next
mother. The same mother. Her son dead.
Her sons dead. Cracks connect them.
Systematically. The killer is many killers.
In different colors and clashing cultures.
Chain murderers packed in suits of
"Bigsby and Kruthers." Bangers with
nothing but bullets. American fascists
parading in jurisprudence. Cracks in the
system hook them up. A deadly circuitry
links them to us. Phone screams stab our
ears in the night, with chronic news of our
warrior children. Poverty their serial killer.
Delivering another child unwanted.
We watch them die young, as they start
to grow wise, threatening to become more
than a gangsta tribe. The loss lives in
Patricia's eyes — tears of their second
mother. The stats of death not safe
this time, hidden in twisted headlines.

These are casualties we know.

Sticking like sights of Oklahoma. Bombed
and crying. Debris rising. Children dying.
Their cities burned down everyday. Ignited
by things they do not own. Detonated by
things denied. They become warriors –
clashing in despair-occupied cemeteries
for a pure breath of life.

Ouija Boards,
Chocolat,
Magnolias

Torturing my Wife

Woke up this morning with my mouth open wide
as an entrance to a cave. My breath a spelunker
rappelling deep into darkness. A mighty, monstrous,
sound reverberating subterraneously, scaring bats
into streams of painful day, forcing stalactites
to crash clamorously to the guano-encrusted rocks.

Patricia claims this racket emanates from my
peaceful lungs. She is insane.

She is hearing in her sleep.

When a tree falls in the forest and you are not there
does it make a sound? What if two of you are in the
forest and the same tree keeps falling every night, but only one
of you hears it? Is the sound really that bad?

Once I really was in the woods.

In the mountains of Atlanta, eighty troubled men and boys,
Luis and I, at the side of Malidoma and Michael Meade.
We were elders drumming under an equinoctial moon.
In the morning Luis claimed I roared. Maybe like a lion.
Maybe like a bear. Maybe like the Blue Nile Falls.

I imagine myself an onyx-glazed 747.

I eject the exhaust of my human engine into the inner ear
of the forest. One morning in a state of quasi-slumber,
I caught myself, for a millisecond, blasting — the cannon
in Tchaikovsky's 1812 Overture. No one else was there.

I lost my reasonable doubt.

The sound of snoring, the denial of noise,
became a metaphor for the shit Patricia puts up with.

French Kisses, Hôtel Le Lionceau, Paris

To Patricia Zamora

We are thick

with the scent of broken *chocolat*
seeping into our melodic senses.

Nude walls, thin as *papier-mâché*,
separate us barely from the

mysteries we feel manifesting
in adjacent rooms.

A Frenchman drips carnal lingo
from a glowing screen, drowning out

our unleashed longing, his foreign
tongue wrapping around

our forbidden rapture.

His gibberish rendered
irrelevant by your sweet sorcery.

Your alchemy changing me
from stone to sugar.

Searching for Hair in Stockholm

Stockholm, Sweden

At the center of its cranium
Stockholm is shiny, white, and bald,
missing the kinky fields of urban cities –
graffiti, course and wavy, crackling
when caught in the teeth of steely stares
through glassy slits of speeding trains.

The city's peaceful veil vandalized
by finger scrawl on a rare dirty window,
like defecation to the pristine walls
of "Fredsgaten," an introverted lane,
vacant in its cleanliness, the glass
defiled with the name "Greatful Dead"
misspelled across almond-colored soot.

Along the edges of Stockholm's
astringent structures, lines of lesions
mark inner-city quarries, razor-thin traces
criss-crossing layered and lifeless ice –
the scattered disruption from a Big Bang's
unwanted progeny destined to create a
diametrically opposed form of life.

A Swede, as pale as fish scales, machine
gunned her suggestions into my mind.
She wanted Stockholm upside-down
hanging by its knees, white from lack of
circulation, drained by her scathing exposé.
Despising silence, even the cotton shroud
she wore narrated her body's story.
She left the train, her own aerosol poems
sprayed in the still Swedish air.

Beautiful Swimmers

New Syrma Beach, Florida

Pull back the head…

Elisenda teaches the art of beheading
enthusiastically. The other composers
face her with lumps in their throats
and crabs between their fingers, like
thick-barbed strings. They all have rhythm
but are woefully out of synch, splattering
flesh across the table in brutal sixteenths.

Open its belly. Pull all that stuff out.

Under the armored apron its gender
revealed — the male's belly "an inverted
T" (a phallus to me) the female broad
as the Venus of Willendorf (a crab
with hips). The master strikes delicacy,
a bloated "sponge crab," its orange eggs
pop like fatty diamonds to suck.

Pull off the arms. Harder…

As if she is stamping flamenco.

Suck out the meat…

As if that instruction is needed.

Toss the gutted body…

Our slop bucket is brimming
with legs, torsos, claws and glorious
but rejected eggs. I soar above
the carnage, rejoicing in my
crablessness and sink my silver spoon
into the table's communal gumbo.

This *is* flamenco.

One of the composers is on top
of our table, her red skirt flowing,
dancing on the cracked apron
of the *Callinectes sapidus,* Greek
for "beautiful swimmer," throwing
morsels of its pale treasure
into our gaping mouths.

Johnny At Diablo

I am the classic Western of your most violent
wet dreams, the golden calf of your pop-cult religion.
My ten-gallon hat, Winchester, and chaps, are stored
on your Smithsonian altar.

I am the hero worship of your war-mongering core.
Every wood-frame town I ride into is an ideological track
into your mind. Every stained glass saloon is the liquid
high between you and your factory grind.

The stubble-jawed miscreant you watch me gun down
in the high-noon heat is more than a common cattle thief.
I am every exploiter you want to flatten with your steel
Dodge sedan loaded with features and plastic explosives.

Every TV game host you wanted gagged and abducted
for putting nothing behind the wrong door. Every landlord
that quadrupled your rent in an orgy of gentrification and
displacement in the name of safety and cleanliness.

I shot the real folk you could not shoot, but wanted to.
I shot them for you. I shot thousands of them. Dressed up
like little brown-skinned banditos. I massacred them with a
six-shooter miraculously loaded with six thousand bullets.

I gave you the fluffy feeling of acceptance allowing you to
fit in with bombings in Managua, Maputo, Hanoi, Powelton,
with the burning of slums and villages, with the witch hunts
and tailored lawns on which students were shot and buried.

I cornered you outside the OK Corral making you believe
you too were a son of Katie Elder. Through me you would

always win. The world just one giant Technicolor Western.
I was the local sheriff – a loaded pistol in my hand.

Performed in the theatre performance "What's This In My Coke?"

Duke Checks Out Ella As She Scats Like That

When Ella starts scatting
      she magnolia planted
beside Duke playing
that tonal Ouija board
and he swings her that slick,
startled, "woman you too
bad" intonation,
      when the Duke do dat,
survival becomes a god
to marvel at, even as the creator
of Mt. Kilimanjaro, survival
transmuted from sanctimonious
sanctioned genocide to African
angels swinging that singing
like a trumpet made
of clouds and lightning, toppling
walls in a way that can only be
called biblical, metaphysical,
in the umbilical between heaven
and Hades, where the devil
is an angel stringing sounds
      that defy atrocity.
When Ella starts scatting
and in an approaching layer
of time Nina Simone wails
of Four Women, after Lady Day
cast southern trees in a bright
white light that not only
dreamily signaled death,
but was death,

and we are majestically
resurrected by Mahalia,
     a miracle happens,
     continues to happen.
More than a mere resurrection,
a triumph over inhumanity.
When Ella starts scatting
'cause the Trumpet man Armstrong
momentarily
then momentously forgot
his words
and spontaneously
started this ingenious tongue
and James Brown
put horns, and strings, and funk,
and things,
a primal electrified scream,
all in the same thing,
thang, thing, thang, thang.
And *Papa's Got A Brand New Bag*
tells us it is never ending, never
ending, always something new
interpenetrating the old
like the digital ripping   off
of the G-Fatha's analog riffs
by the hip-hopping Cab
Calloways of today,
a ghettoized tribute
to his funknosity,
to global tenacity,
to the Yoruba way, that lives
in every beat
and b-note created
by our creators,
when Ella scats
like that...

Acknowledgments

I GIVE MY GRATITUDE to the poets who helped to nurture many of these poems. The shaping and shearing of the raw work benefited especially from the critical eyes of Adrienne Rich, Reginald Gibbons, Patricia Smith, Lucy Anderton, Bob Holman, Quincy Troupe, and Chicago workshop members Julie Parson Nesbitt, Elise Paschen, and Li Young Lee. I am indebted to my life-long friend Luis Rodriguez for the difference he continues to make through his vision, commitment, and sharp skills. It is a gift to again have my poems wrapped up under the covers of Tia Chucha Press and the exquisite and eye-popping art of Tony Fitzpatrick and design of Jane Brunette. Praise to Jack Hirschman for the first publication and translation of my poetry and to the late great Gwendolyn Brooks for her early recognition and that first literary award. I thank the National Endowment for the Arts for its support of both the writing and publication of these poems. Patricia Zamora has lived with the creation, agonizing, celebration, and culmination of this undertaking. Both the poetry and I are better because of her insight, encouragement, patience, and love.

Grateful acknowledgment is made for the following poems:

"Duke Checks Out Ella As She Scats Like That" was published in *TriQuarterly (Special Section: Twenty American Poets), 1996*, at *PoetrySpeaks.com*, 2009 and in *Volume I. Revolutionary Poets Brigade (Caza de Poesia), 2010*.

"Serow" was published at *PoetrySpeaks.com*, 2009 and in *Volume I. Revolutionary Poets Brigade (Caza de Poesia), 2010*.

"Man Within the Boy," "My Father's Favorite Pastime, " "Back to Baton Rouge," "Street Signs, Convolutions, and Other California Coincidences," "A Naivety Scene," and "Torturing My Wife," were published at *PoetrySpeaks.com*, 2009.

"Hallucinating at the Velvet Lounge" and "First Time Ever," were published at *PoetrySpeaks.com* and recorded on *the space of in between* (recording by Nefasha Ayer), 2009.

"Plotting At the Ras Hotel — Addis Ababa" was published in *Warpland — A Journal of Black Literature and Ideas*, (Chicago State University), 1996 and at *PoetrySpeaks.com*, 2009.

"Gravitas – In Three Movements (For Fred Fine)" *was* published at About.com (Poetry), 2006 and in *The Spoken Word Revolution Redux* (SourceBooks), 2007.

"Truth Incinerated" was published at *Poets Against War.com*, 2007.

"Warriors" was published in *Power Lines: A Decade of Poetry From Chicago's Guild Complex* (Tia Chucha Press), 1999 and *Expressions of Englewood*, 2007.

"Her Words (To Gwendolyn Brooks)" was published in *TriQuarterly (Special Section: Twenty American Poets), 1996.*

"Malcolm Is 'Bout More Than Wearing A Cap" was published in *Unsettling America: Race and Ethnicity in Contemporary American Poetry* (Viking/Penguin), 1994, *River Styx,* 1995 and at *PoetrySpeaks.com*, 2009.

"An Open Letter To Clarence Thomas" was published in *Contemporary US Poems of Protest (Le Temps Des CeRises)*, 1997.

"Johnny at Diablo" was published in *Poetry for Peace* (The Peace Museum), 1996.

"The Theory of Subtlety" was published in *River Styx*, 1995, and *The Baffler*, University of Chicago, 1996.

"Poem Inspired By A Crazed Negro Nazi," was published in *River Styx*, 1996.

"Searching For Hair in Stockholm" was published in *New American Writing* and in *Hamburger Ziegel — Jahrbach fur Literatur IV 1995/96.*

"Manchild" was published in *Jackleg Press, 1996* and *Hamburger Ziegel — Jahrbach fur Literatur IV 1995/96.*

"French Kisses" was published in *Jackleg Press, 1996.*

"Number 3 King Drive" and "Sometimes I See Me In That Alley," were published in *Hamburger Ziegel — Jahrbach fur Literatur IV 1995/96.*

"Nazar Picks Me Up" was published in *River Styx*, 1996.

"Stealing Souls," "Revolutionary Eyes," Desert Lost," and "Finger Language," were published as "What Are You Doing Here? A Translation of Unheard Thoughts" in *Literati Internazionale*, Vol. 1, No. 1. (McGraw-Beauchamp Publications/Southern Illinois University), 1991.